# A Bible in Your Backpack

Devotions to Experience Christ in Nature

Donald Wollenhaupt

New Harbor Press

RAPID CITY, SD

Wollenhaupt/New Harbor Press
1601 Mt. Rushmore Rd. Ste 3288
Rapid City, SD 57701
www.NewHarborPress.com

A Bible in Your Backpack / Donald Wollenhaupt. -- 1st ed.
ISBN 978-1-63357-223-2

*To Kimberly, my beautiful and supportive wife;*
*to my son Andrew, my mighty warrior for God; and*
*to my daughter Sofia, my joyful observer of nature.*
*May you continue to enjoy the fullness of God and His Creation.*

# Contents

A Bible in Your Backpack

# Introduction

**Amusement or Amazement**

A friend came back from a trip to a major amusement park in Florida. Being thrifty, she was frustrated with the high cost of the parking, entry fee, and food and drink. The day of her visit was hot and muggy, the lines were long, and air conditioning could only be found at shows or rides that she wasn't interested in. As she tried to relax on a bench, she watched young families laden with ice cream, sodas, and toys. She started adding up the costs and was horrified at how much these families were spending. She left tired, dehydrated (because even the drinks were too high priced), and with much emptier pockets—fully convinced that the day wasn't worth it. For her, it had been a long day of "amusement."

In contrast, a visit to a national park may incur a very minimal entrance fee and will provide a variety of activities for fun, health, and hands-on learning. In addition, eating a healthy picnic lunch while enjoying the plants and wildlife within the park is refreshing and inexpensive.

The comparison between the joy of being in nature and the "fun" of an amusement park is striking to me! Amusement parks have their merits. They provide a family fun day of entertainment, and, for some, a once in a lifetime "bucket list" activity. However, amusement parks are not on my bucket list. I'm not a fan of roller coasters, waiting in long lines, or eating cotton candy. A jog in a park, viewing wildlife, paddling a canoe on a smooth misty morning lake, or cross-country skiing in the woods near sunset is my preference. Naturalist John Muir once said, "In every walk with nature one receives far more than he seeks."

In this devotional, I have written about natural aspects of God's amazing creation and of how nature can remind us of important truths for our lives as Christians.

# Two of my Passions: Nature and Knowing God

Growing up on a farm in southwest Iowa, I was surrounded by many acres of rolling pastures, fields, woods, creeks, and wetlands. There were many farm animals as well as geese, ducks, and colorful pheasants. Although there were plenty of chores, such as working in the cornfields, gardening, hauling hay, and gathering eggs, we would find time to relax in the evenings, playing baseball and chasing lightning bugs. Each day on the farm was its own adventure.

While attending the University of Nebraska majoring in education, I was introduced to a former park ranger. He suggested checking out job opportunities with the national parks. Most people that I knew thought park rangers "climbed fire towers" keeping an eye out for forest fires in the Pacific West. The park ranger helped me through the complicated federal application process, and I received a job as a campground ranger at Shenandoah National Park in Virginia. I am still grateful to that friend who helped start me out on a lifelong career.

I worked in several national parks, national historic sites, and national recreation areas across the United States. I delivered educational talks, took park visitors on nature hikes, and gave tours of historic sites. For the last half of my career, I worked as the Chief of Education in the Southeast Regional Office in Atlanta, advising the education operations for 66 parks in the southeastern United States and the Caribbean. I also traveled on six international assignments to assist other countries with education programs in their national parks. During my 38 years with the park service, I had a passion for the natural and historical resources of the parks and a desire to share this passion with park visitors.

My life on a farm and working in parks taught me that the natural environment can provide a refuge from daily activities; a place of refreshment to value God's creation; a safe haven for physical, mental, and spiritual healing; and last, but not least, an opportunity to enjoy life experiences with God in nature.

However there are things in nature that are not so pleasant: air pollution, water pollution, and unsightly litter. Just like contaminants that mess-up the environment, sin pollutes our minds and souls. They are harmful to us as we desire a fulfilling relationship with God and with one another. Our enemy, Satan, wants to get us distracted and take us off the path. God desires us to enjoy the spiritual path that He has prepared for us. A path that acknowledges sin and leads to repentance so that we may live in the fullness of love, joy, and relationship with Him.

My greatest passions are knowing and serving God, and sharing His love, forgiveness, and salvation with others. It is my passion for Christ that kindles a compassionate heart for others in me. I want to live a life worthy of God and tell others about the love of Christ. As a park ranger, I felt I was a "missionary for our parks." God has also led me to be a witness for Him. I am not a theologian, seminary student, or someone who has written a lot of books on faith and religion. I am just an ordinary guy, a former park ranger, and a person who loves God—the One who created it all for us to care for and enjoy.

Following are 52 devotions that link my experiences in nature with a glimpse into God's character and power—helping me overcome temptation and keeping me on the right path with Jesus. So let's place a Bible in our backpacks as together we take a hike through nature each week and look at Scriptures to help guide us on our journey.

# Week 1:   Waterfalls - God's Power

> As His divine power has given to us all things that pertain to life and godliness, through the knowledge of Him who called us by glory and virtue. - 2 Peter 1:3

When you stand and watch a waterfall, what words run through your mind? Perhaps awesome, stunning, or powerful. Waterfalls amaze me as they cascade downward to the river below. I am struck by the height of the falls, the amount of water rushing over the edge, and the thunderous sound that is made as the falling water hits the water below.

There are many beautiful waterfalls in the world. You may have seen some of the better known ones—Niagara Falls on the U.S./Canadian border, Yellowstone Falls in Yellowstone National Park, or even Victoria Falls between Zambia and Zimbabwe. One of my international assignments with the park service was to assist the Protection Areas Commission of Guyana in South America in its tourism efforts. I spent a week at Kaieteur National Park, the site of Kaieteur Falls, which boasts a straight drop of 741 feet. I was impressed not only by the beauty of the waterfall, but by its power as well.

When I watch a waterfall, I am reminded of three of the certainties we have in Christ—the power of His blood over sin, the power of His resurrection, and the power of His forgiveness. God's divine power has "given us all things that pertain to life and godliness." God also showed His power by giving us everlasting life. "But if the Spirit of Him who raised Jesus from the dead dwells in you, He who raised Christ from the dead will also give life to your mortal bodies through His Spirit who dwells in you." (Romans 8:11)

So, next time you are standing near a powerful waterfall, take time to allow these Scriptures to "cascade" in your mind. Be thankful for God's power that helps you to overcome sin and temptation as you live the Christian life.

Admire the power of the Lord in all you see in nature this week.

# Week 2: Bald Eagles - Waiting on the Lord

But those who wait on the Lord shall renew their strength; they shall mount up with wings like eagles. They shall run and not be weary. They shall walk and not faint. - Isaiah 40:31

Symbolizing freedom, the bald eagle is America's national bird. With its distinctive white head and yellow-hooked beak, it flies higher than any other bird, soaring and gliding with little effort. I am always amazed at the eagle's patience as it sits in the trees attentively observing its surroundings. Then in an instant, it sights its prey and springs up effortlessly gaining momentum as it takes flight. When it mounts up in flight, its great strength can be seen.

The first bald eagle I ever saw in flight was in St. Louis, Missouri while working as a park ranger at Gateway Arch National Park. The eagle was majestic and soared effortlessly above the Mississippi River. Wow, that was awesome! I wanted to stop the car and take a longer look.

A number of years later, I worked farther north on the river at a national park called Effigy Mounds National Monument, located on the high bluffs of northeast Iowa. Dozens of bald eagles gathered in the winter feeding along the river's edge. One winter day, I counted at least 50 eagles in the trees along the river or in flight. Although I have seen many eagles since then, seeing a bald eagle is still an awesome experience to me!

The eagle's patience as it anticipates the opportunity for flight impresses me. This patience reminds me of Psalm 130:5, "I wait for the Lord, my soul waits, and in His word I do hope."

Waiting is often a place where our hearts become anxious and our strength is diminished. As we face an unknown future, we often respond with fear. But waiting on the Lord is very different. We prayerfully wait in anticipation of His answer. When we trust in His timing and direction, our strength is renewed. Our hope is in Him. We will "mount up with wings like eagles."

Enjoy a walk in nature this week and wait on the Lord to renew your strength. If you see a bald eagle, admire its wings as it soars in the sky above.

# Week 3: The Desert - Reverence and Quiet

*Be still, and know that I am God.* - Psalm 46:10

When I look out over a desert with its variety of cacti, shrubs, and wildlife, I am amazed at the life that thrives in this hot and dry environment. I especially enjoy the Sonoran Desert of the southwestern United States and northwestern Mexico. I particularly admire its iconic symbol—the tall Saguaro cacti. With their unique treelike arms bending upward, these cacti survive and thrive in the desert's harsh environment for up to 150 to 200 years.

While visiting Saguaro National Park near Tucson, Arizona, I stood still and stared silently out at the desert. An amazing quietness was all around me. "Be still and know that I am God" spoke deeply to my heart. I basked in knowing that God was my Creator and my Lord. I also thought about how God desired for His people to live "quiet and peaceable" lives even in the midst of hardship as referenced in I Timothy 2:2. As I looked at the Saguaro cacti, I offered a prayer of thanksgiving, knowing that God stands tall and watches over me. I was grateful for that very special time with Jesus.

We often face harsh circumstances just like the cacti. Life on earth is often challenging. However, God says, "Fear not, for I am with you; be not dismayed, for I am your God. I will strengthen you, yes, I will help you, I will uphold you with My righteous right hand." (Isaiah 41:10) Because of His love and care for us, we too can survive and even thrive through those challenging times. We can therefore draw near to Him in prayer and with reverence.

Make nature part of your week. Know that the Lord is God.
If you happen to be in the Southwest, please take time to
experience the peace and quiet the desert affords.

# Week 4: A Free-Flowing Stream - The Refreshing Spirit of God

Purge me with hyssop, and I shall be clean; wash me, and I shall be whiter than snow … Create in me a clean heart, O God, and renew a steadfast spirit within me. - Psalm 51:7,10

It is a hot summer day, and I am out for a jog running beside a free-flowing stream. Sweat is pouring down my face, and my legs are tired. I need a break. The stream with its cool, flowing water is inviting, so I wade into it. I am refreshed both physically and mentally, and head back out on the trail again to finish my run.

Relieving tired muscles in a cool stream is an excellent recovery method after a run. Distance runners use this approach to reduce the amount of inflammation in their legs. I often find that not only do I need restoration as a runner, but I also need restoration in my Christian walk.

Psalm 51 was written by King David after he sinned greatly. He acknowledged his sin, asked to be cleansed, and then desired to be restored to the joy of God's salvation. Like David, once we repent of our sins and ask for forgiveness, He "creates a clean heart" in us and "renews a steadfast spirit" within us. It's like wading into a cool, flowing stream and coming out spiritually refreshed.

One of my favorite verses is John 3:16, "For God so loved the world that He gave His only begotten Son, that whoever believes in Him should not perish but have everlasting life." Have you believed in Jesus and invited Him to be Lord of your life? If not, prayerfully seek Him. Below is a prayer that may express your heart:

Dear Lord Jesus, I know that I am a sinner, and I ask for Your forgiveness. I believe You died for my sins and rose from the dead. I confess and turn from my sins, and invite you to come into my heart and life. I trust in You as my Savior and Lord. In Jesus' name. Amen.

If you prayed for Jesus to become your Savior and Lord, please communicate this with another Christian. Have joy in your adventure of growing in relationship with Christ.

Take a walk beside a stream this week and enjoy the free-flowing love of God.

# Week 5: Pure Snow - Make Me White as Snow

Blessed are the pure in heart, for they shall see God. - Matthew 5:8

I grew up in the Midwest and attended college in Omaha, Nebraska. Cold, snowy winters were part of life. I enjoyed the pure beauty of the snow as it covered the fields and pastures. I loved to cross-county ski around lakes or along rivers, watching red foxes scamper about the snow-covered forest or noticing bald eagles hanging out in the trees over an ice-covered river. I even found pleasure in jogging in the evening when puffy white snowflakes would fall gently on the ground.

However, winters could be cold, long, and stressful. I had to deal with snow and ice-covered roads—worried that my car could spin out on slick roads and end up stuck in a ditch. Been there; done that! At times it seemed as if I was continually scraping ice and frost off the windshield. In spite of these difficulties, I still found pleasure and delight in being outdoors on a snowy winter day.

A snow-covered landscape reminds me that my heart can be cleansed by Jesus so that I am "whiter than snow." (Psalm 51:7) It's my desire to be as pure as fresh-fallen snow in my daily walk with Him. I pray that He makes us pure and finds us "without blemish and without spot" (I Peter 1:19), just like a snow-covered landscape. Jesus said, "Blessed are the pure in heart, for they shall see God." We can pray that God would work in us a pure heart.

Make nature part of your week and desire that the Holy Spirit work in you a heart that is pure like fresh-fallen snow.

# Week 6: Hiking Paths - Staying on God's Path

*Your word is a lamp to my feet and a light to my path.* - Psalm 119:105

Most national parks have maintained hiking trails, providing a link for the visitor to the park's natural and historical features as well as to their recreational opportunities. The marked trails benefit visitors by providing safe paths and clear direction. The trails also provide protection to the surrounding plants and wildlife. While hiking, it's easy to get distracted by the beauty of the landscape or by wanting to get a closer look at wildlife. It's tempting to be lured off the path. Once off the path, we are in danger of damaging the ecosystem, becoming lost, or even sustaining an injury.

Before heading out on a hike, we need to prepare our backpacks. Here are some items we may need:

- Provisions (a trail map, a compass, a first aid kit, sun protection, rain gear, a change of clothes, matches, a flashlight, and a knife);
- Sustenance (food and water); and
- Connections (a cell phone, a back-up battery, and your Bible—also, make sure someone knows your hiking plans).

With these essentials in mind, what provisions, sustenance, and connections do we need in our walk with God? As the psalmist wrote, God's "Word is a lamp unto our feet and a light unto our path." Referring to the Bible we have placed in our backpacks regularly keeps us on God's path in this life. The devil is well aware of what it takes for us to become distracted with worldly things. The leading of the Holy Spirit (provisions),

Scriptures (sustenance), and prayer (connections) help us to focus on the path we are on.

Enjoy your time in nature this week as you walk on the trail. Be prepared with the essentials for a Godly life and for your hike in nature.

# Week 7: Armored Animals - The Armor of God

*Put on the full armor of God, so that you can take your stand against the devil's schemes. - Ephesians 6:11*

Some animals have "armor" or a protective system to keep them safe from the attack of predators. Five that stand out to me are armadillos, porcupines, rhinos, skunks, and turtles. Armadillos have a leathery shell that protects them from most natural predators. The sharp spines or quills of the porcupine deter the curious. Skunks, as some of us have experienced, emit a strong and unpleasant smell that keeps predators at bay. And the bony shell of a turtle acts as a shield against intruders. The rhinoceros has the most impressive "armor" to me with its extremely thick skin, imposing size, and deadly horn. I don't think many animals or humans want to tangle with a rhinoceros!

What can we humans do to to defend ourselves against the often subtle and devious attacks of Satan? We need armor. Spiritually speaking, we do have protective armor - God's armor - as described in Ephesians 6:13-18: "Therefore take up the **whole armor of God**, that you may be able to withstand in the evil day, and having done all, to stand. Stand therefore, having **girded your waist** with truth, having put on the **breastplate** of righteousness, and having **shod your feet** with the preparation of the gospel of peace; above all, taking the **shield** of faith with which you will be able to quench all the fiery darts of the wicked one. And take the **helmet** of salvation, and the **sword** of the Spirit, which is the word of God; praying always with all prayer and supplication in the Spirit, being watchful to this end with all perseverance and supplication for all the saints." As I say these verses, I will often move my hands as though I am putting on the armor of God. Thank you, God, for the amazing armor you have given us.

Enjoy your time in nature this week and put on your protective gear—the whole armor of God.

# Week 8: The Mysterious Ocean - Our Amazing and Unfathomable God

> "For My thoughts are not your thoughts, nor are your ways My ways," says the Lord. "For as the heavens are higher than the earth, so are My ways higher than your ways, and My thoughts than your thoughts." - Isaiah 55:8-9

I remember when I saw the ocean for the first time at Fort Lauderdale Beach on Florida's Atlantic coast. Growing up, we were very busy on the farm, and the only vacations my family took were to the Iowa State Fair in Des Moines. So, when I saw the ocean for the first time, I was totally mesmerized. I wondered how far it was before the ocean dipped below the horizon. I also wondered how pelicans flew so effortlessly as they skimmed quietly and smoothly across the top of the ocean's water.

Although I've now seen several of the world's oceans and seas, I am still mesmerized by the ocean. While we are able to delight in and even understand many aspects of the ocean, it still remains a mystery. Many mysteries remain about the ocean—among them are its salty substance, its myriad of creatures, its sea floor, and its vast expanses.

Just like there is much unknown about the oceans, there is also much we don't know about the thoughts of God. As Job 1:7 says, "Can you search out the deep things of God? Can you find out the limits of the Almighty?" His ways are truly beyond our comprehension. Some of the truths that we can't fully understand are that the One who created all things would chose to live among us (John 1:14); that Christ died for us while we were still sinners (Romans 5:8); and that the Holy Spirit has been given to us and will abide with us forever (John 14:16). The revelation of His love for us is even more unfathomable than the oceans. What an opportunity we have to delve into the Word and learn more about Him!

Enjoy your time in nature this week and take time to learn more about our amazing God. Plan a trip to the ocean to enjoy its beauty and mystery.

# Week 9:   The Night Sky - Navigating Life

The heavens declare the glory of God; and the firmament shows His handiwork. - Psalm 19:1

While we value nature here on earth, we also can enjoy looking above at the night sky. The sky offers us some exciting glimpses of nature beyond our own planet. My wife is a night-sky enthusiast. She is often out on our back deck looking at the stars and planets, identifying constellations, and sometimes looking at the planets or the moon through her telescope.

While driving at night in Oklahoma many years ago, we took a wrong turn off the main road and discovered that we were lost. Those were the days before GPS or Google maps so we didn't even know what direction we were heading. My wife pointed to the constellation Orion and determined that we were heading west instead of south as we should have been. We turned south and soon found the main road we needed. The night sky, God's navigational tool, showed us the way home!

At the time of Jesus birth, three wise men navigated by the stars to find the baby Jesus in Bethlehem and bring Him gifts. God used the stars to guide these men to His Son. Throughout time, explorers have used the stars to navigate their way around the world. The outstretched expanse of the sky has shown God's handiwork to many generations.

The Bible is our navigator for all aspects of life. Every time we go to His Word, the Bible helps to navigate and to lead us. When we need direction in our lives, the Scriptures guide us. When we need healing and comfort, His Word gives us hope. When we feel down and discouraged, His Word encourages us. The Scriptures, along with the Holy Spirit, daily guide us to stay on the right course and lead us toward our eternal home with Jesus. Speaking through the psalmist, God said, "I will instruct you and teach you in the way you should go; I will counsel you with my eye upon you." (Psalm 32:8)

As you gaze on the night sky this week, reflect on the way our God "navigates" in your life.

# Week 10:  Cedar Trees - Endurance

> Not only so, but we also glory in our sufferings, because we know that suffering produces perseverance; perseverance, character; and character, hope. - Romans 5:3-4 (NIV)

Cedar trees have historically symbolized strength and endurance. They are incredibly strong, endure harsh weather, and live for many years. Because of their strength and resilience, cedar trees are used as windbreaks for farms, residences, and sometimes in nature preserves. While other trees may fall prey to storms and constant unrelenting winds, cedar trees are resistant to those fierce winds and storms. After many years, they may look weathered and worn, yet they endure, standing strong through the test of time. The wood of the cedar tree also has a strong spicy fragrance that lasts for many years. I like lifting the top of a cedar chest just to smell the aroma of the wood.

The unrelenting winds that buffet cedar trees remind us of the often relentless winds of difficulties and temptations in our lives. Only with the power of the Holy Spirit in us can we resist being overtaken and can we patiently endure in the face of adversity. Rejoicing in our suffering is usually not our immediate response. Yet Romans 5:3-4 reveals that we can rejoice in suffering, because of what it produces in us.

Discouragement does not need to be the outcome of our suffering. Instead the outcome should be hope. For we know that in Christ, suffering leads to endurance and develops character in us, and that leads to hope. What an amazing and God-given outcome! During the darkest times of our lives, we can remember the endurance of the cedar trees as hope is produced in us!

In 2 Corinthians 2:14-15, Paul says, "Now thanks be to God who always leads us in triumph in Christ, and through us diffuses the fragrance of His knowledge in every place. For we are to God the fragrance of Christ." In my life, this "fragrance of Christ" is clearest when I have walked with and learned to trust and hope in Him through difficult times. Like the cedar tree that has a long-lasting fragrance, we too can spread the "fragrance of His knowledge" as we learn to stand firm and dependent on Him.

Enjoy your walk in nature this week. Experience the fragrance of Christ, and find comfort, strength, and hope in God even during difficult times.

# Week 11: The Reflection on a Crystal Clear Lake - Reflecting Jesus

Let your light so shine before men, that they may see your good works and glorify your Father in heaven. - Matthew 5:16

If you hike around a lake, you often will see a striking reflection of the natural landscape on the lake. I admire the reflected beauty, and like many of us, take a photograph. However on rainy or windy days, the surface of the water shows a distorted reflection or no reflection at all.

Like the lake reflecting the mountains, the surface of our lives "reflects" what is deeper—what is in our hearts. What am I reflecting? Am I reflecting the character of Jesus? What do people see in me? Do they see a clear reflection of patience, kindness, generosity, and love? Or do they instead see impatience, unkindness, greed, or, worse, a sinful judgmental attitude?

I know there are days when I fail to reflect Christ's love. I let something obscure the reflection. Sometimes I am walking through turbulent or stormy times in my own life. All of us experience difficult challenges in life, such as illness, financial need, or concerns for a family member. Sometimes the "reflection" is not clear because of choices that I have made that are not in line with His Word or His leading. But these issues do not need to obscure the love of Jesus in my heart.

I continually pray that I would draw closer to Jesus through the difficult times and receive His peace and rest. I pray that I would be willing to repent when I have strayed from His path. I also pray that I would seek His will, and that His love would be reflected ever more brightly in my life. I want to imitate and reflect what is good and not evil, so that I can encourage others in their walk with God. My hope is that others see these "good works," and glorify the Father in heaven.

As you enjoy your walk in nature this week, pray and seek ways that you may reflect His nature and love to others.

# Week 12:   A Pile of Stones
# - Refrain from
# Casting Judgment

So when they continued asking Him, He raised
Himself up and said to them, "He who is without
sin among you, let him throw a stone at her first."
- John 8:7

In one of the most pointed stories in the Bible, the teachers
of the Jewish law brought a women who had sinned to Jesus.
They said to Him that according to the law, the women should
be stoned, and they waited to see what Jesus would say.
Jesus responded, "He who is without sin among you, let him
throw a stone at her first." They all turned and left. No one in
the crowd was without sin.

When I see a pile of stones, I often think of this story. The
stones remind me that because of my own sins, I have no right
to pick up any stones in judgment of others. When I am being
critical and accusing someone, my judgmental attitude hurts
them—just like a stone that is thrown! It also hardens my own
heart. Instead, I need to confess my own sin, and then show
compassion to those who struggle with sin around me.

All of us have habits and obstacles that hold us back, but we
tend to see the sin in others more readily than in ourselves.
Matthew 7:3 clearly warns us, "And why do you look at the
speck in your brother's eye, but do not consider the plank
in your own eye?" Satan cleverly uses our self-centered
nature to magnify others' mistakes and keeps us from paying
attention to our own faults and sins.

We are all on this path together. So casting any stones is
placing us off God's path. We need to repent and turn from
our own sins, and seek how God would have us help other -
"casting" compassion toward people instead of judgment.

Make nature part of your week. Leave the pile of stones and any judgmental attitude alone.

# Week 13: The American Robin - Coming of a New Season in Christ

Therefore we do not lose heart. Even though our outward man is perishing, yet the inward man is being renewed day by day. For our light affliction, which is but for a moment, is working for us a far more exceeding and eternal weight of glory."
- 2 Corinthians 4:16-17

Winter—it has its own natural beauty. The snow-covered landscape can be very picturesque. It is a time for much of nature to rest and to hibernate. Growing up in Iowa, I loved to be outdoors in the winter with activities, such as snowshoeing or running in the bright afternoon sun. My brother and I played hockey games on frozen ponds and jumped in large snowdrifts as often as we could.

However, wintry weather, with ice-covered roads, slippery sidewalks, and blowing and drifting snow made travel, or even just walking outside, hazardous. The mix of snow, sleet, ice, and freezing rain was particularly dangerous. Winters in Iowa lasted from November through most of March and sometimes into April. During the long winters, I would wonder if spring and warm weather would ever come. Finally, things would begin to warm up. The snow would start to melt; the frozen streams, to thaw; the trees, to bud; and robins appeared. The sight of the first robin meant the cold, hard winter was nearly over, and a new season was beginning.

The American robin with its reddish-orange breast and bright singing reminds us that even though things may still look cold and dreary, there is hope for the future. With spring and its robins, God provides a new season of warmth and growth, and a reminder that we can look forward to renewed hope for the future. "Therefore we [should] not lose heart" even while things may seem bleak. God "is working for us a far more exceeding and eternal weight of glory."

Life's circumstances, like an extended winter season, may delay a "new spring" season in our life. Therefore, we need to stay steadfast in the Lord and focus on our eternal reward in Christ. Then today's circumstances will not succeed in diminishing our hope. Our hope remains in the Lord.

Enjoy a time in nature this week. If you see a robin, thank God for the renewed hope you have in Him.

# Week 14: Dodging Rainstorms - Finding Refuge from the Storm

Whoever dwells in the shelter of the Most High will rest in the shadow of the Almighty. I will say of the LORD, "He is my refuge and my fortress, my God, in whom I trust." - Psalm 91:1-2 (NIV)

In west Texas, the vistas go on for miles and miles. While driving on Route I-40 outside Amarillo, I saw a huge rain cloud just north of the road about a quarter of a mile away. It looked like it was raining buckets. Thankfully, I was traveling parallel to the rainstorm, and the rain stayed to my left.

As I periodically glanced to my left at the storm, I was reminded that God is my refuge in the storm, and I felt comfortable even though there was a huge storm that could overtake me. To me, it was a visual representation of the protection that I have in God. As Psalm 36:7 says, "How precious is Your lovingkindness, O God! Therefore the children of men put their trust under the shadow of Your wings."

In life, some days are sunny and warm, while other days are overcast and then sometimes a cloudburst hits. Most of us have faced such times; often life is not easy. Difficulties and temptations flare up and hit us like a harsh rainstorm. If our eyes aren't fixed on Jesus, we begin to worry or can even be overwhelmed by the circumstances in our lives.

On that drive in west Texas, I wasn't overtaken by the storm, but many times I have felt quite overwhelmed in my life. Regardless of my circumstances, I can remember that God is my refuge and fortress and that His steadfast love gives me the shelter that I need through life's storms. When we place our lives and our trust in Him, we can dwell in the comfort and refuge of the Lord.

Remember that God is your refuge as you walk in nature this week.

# Week 15:   Tailgrass Prairies - Living in Harmony

> Now may the God of patience and comfort grant you to be like-minded toward one another, according to Christ Jesus. - Romans 15:5

Tallgrass prairies are one of my favorite ecosystems. Prairies, also called grasslands, are perhaps America's rarest and most diverse ecosystems. At one time, the American prairie covered most of the Great Plains from Illinois to Colorado and from the prairie provinces of Canada to Texas.

In the early 1800s, farmers who settled the prairie found the root system and the density of plants difficult to turn into farmland—that is, until the steel-bladed plow was invented by John Deere in 1837. Due to this invention and related farming practices, less than 4% of the original prairie is now left. The once vast prairie of the Midwest Plains is now the breadbasket of America. In recognition of its importance, the U.S. Congress established the Tallgrass Prairie National Preserve in Kansas to protect "a nationally significant remnant of the once vast tallgrass prairie ecosystem." (https://www.nps.gov/tapr/index.htm)

Prairies are a complex ecosystem offering some of the most stunning scenes in nature. In these thick grasslands, an abundance of plants, birds, wildlife, and insects live in harmony with one another. In spring, wildflowers are vibrant, and, in summer, the tallgrasses look like waves of green and yellow in the prairie meadow. In autumn, I particularly enjoy seeing the hawks and meadowlarks on the fenceposts. And in winter, the prairie plants and wildlife seem to take a rest, but the prairie is still a great place for a hiking adventure.

The natural harmony of the prairie ecosystem is a constant reminder to me of the spiritual harmony that should exist between Christians. It reminds me that we should make every effort to "keep the unity of the Spirit in the bond of peace." (Ephesians 4:3) We should endeavor to live in harmony with other Christian brothers and sisters, and help others live and thrive in God's created world.

This week notice the harmony in God's creation. If you are traveling through the Midwest or Great Plains, stop at a prairie park and enjoy its natural harmony.

# Week 16: Enjoying Fruit - Taste and See that the Lord is Good

Oh, taste and see that the Lord is good; blessed is the man who trusts in Him! - Psalm 34:8

I love fruit of any type—they are healthy, natural treats. I try to eat at least three or four pieces of fruit a day. There are so many choices, such as a Florida orange, a Hawaiian pineapple, Maine blueberries, or a Georgia peach. Also, a banana with strawberries blended into a smoothie with wildflower honey is a tasty treat. What great nutritional snacks God has given us. Just the thought of these makes me hungry!

When I eat an apple or a handful of grapes, I want to fully enjoy it. Too often, however, I gulp the fruit down in a hurry, and then think, why did I eat that piece of fruit so quickly? What I should have done is taken my time, and given thanks for those who planted, picked, and sent the fruit to market. I also should have savored each bite thinking of its goodness, and what it would mean to my health.

Just like the fruit, how often do I quickly read over a verse and mentally "gulp down" the Scriptures without really thinking about what I just read or its meaning to me? Isn't His Word meant for my well-being and nourishment? What is God saying in those words for me? The Scriptures are more than just words. I should take my time reading Scripture—really "tasting" it, meditating on it, understanding it, and applying it to my life. I need to appreciate all that God has done for me and savor the Scriptures as nourishment for my soul.

Take time to "taste and see that the Lord is good" and mix in some fruitful Scriptures as you walk in nature this week.

# Week 17: Access on the River - Access to God the Father Through Jesus Christ

Therefore, having been justified by faith, we have peace with God through our Lord Jesus Christ, through whom also we have access by faith into this grace in which we stand, and rejoice in hope of the glory of God. - Romans 5:1-2

Canoeing or rafting on one of our beautiful waterways is a wonderful adventure. Paddling a canoe on a smooth serene lake early in the morning when the mist can be seen rising off the water is a cool, calming experience. Rafting down a free-flowing river can be a quite different and thrilling experience. Both require work by those paddling—one to move the canoe along the water and the other to get through the rapids on the river. But before the adventure can start, you need to find an access point—a safe place to launch the canoe or raft.

This reminds me of the access that has been provided to us through Jesus Christ our Savior. Jesus said, "I am the way, the truth, and the life. No one comes to the Father except through Me." (John 14:6) We gained unprecedented access to God by Jesus' blood on the cross. We can now "stand, and rejoice in hope of the glory of God." Because of His grace, we have the privilege to come close to Him and grow in Him as we walk the Christian life.

It is interesting that once I gain access on the water or with God, I don't have to worry about gaining access again. I continue paddling, enjoying the natural beauty and spiritual journey before me. I am grateful for the many experiences and for the joy of being in nature and with God. This life with Christ would not have been possible if access to God through Jesus Christ had not been provided for my journey.

Enjoy nature this week and the access God has given to us by the grace of our Lord Jesus Christ.

# Week 18:  A Flock of Cedar Waxwings - Blessings from God

> For God so loved the world that He gave His only begotten Son, that whoever believes in Him should not perish but have everlasting life. - John 3:16

I enjoy watching birds in our backyard. Cardinals, chickadees, goldfinches, woodpeckers and thrashers, to name a few, visit our backyard and bird feeders. One day I noticed a flock of Cedar Waxwings in the trees—what an amazing scene! I had always been fascinated by this striking bird. As a child, I had painted a plastic model of a Cedar Waxwing, but had never seen a real one. Now there was not just one, but an entire flock of Cedar Waxwings in my backyard! It felt like God just wanted to say, "Here is a gift—a blessing from me to show you how much I care about you and the desires of your heart."

I realize this may seem trivial, after all, it was just a flock of birds. But it was something I had always desired to see. Sometimes it's the simple pleasures from God that remind us to be grateful for the many blessings that the Lord has given. God desires good for us. He blesses us day in and day out. These blessings can be answers to prayers for our spouse, children, grandchildren, treasured friends, livelihood, or continued health. These blessings can also come in smaller packages like the Cedar Waxwings, a beautiful sunset on the beach, or receiving an encouraging note from a friend during a difficult time.

A most treasured blessing from our gracious God is His promise of eternal life to those who believe in Jesus. Luke 12:32 says, "Do not fear little flock, for it is your Father's good pleasure to give you the kingdom." It is His desire to give us this treasured gift—to be with Him forever. The Lord knows that we have doubts, fears, and uncertainties in our lives. When Jesus returned to the Father, He sent the Holy Spirit to be with us as our Comforter and Helper as mentioned in John 14:16. So we have the blessing of the Holy Spirit in this life and the promise of eternal life with Him in the next. I am truly grateful to God for His many blessings.

Enjoy your walk in nature this week. Count how many types of birds you see and count God's many blessings—great and small.

# Week 19:   Loving Nature ... an Idol?

> You shall not make for yourself a carved image [idol]—any likeness of anything that is in heaven above, or that is in the earth beneath, or that is in the water under the earth. - Exodus 20:4

When I mention nature and its connection to God, and how nature reminds me of applying Scriptures to my life, sometimes I get a response like, "Don, are you one of those nature worshippers?" This is perhaps a question worth considering. I do get excited when I see a bald eagle in flight, a cascading waterfall, or a free-flowing stream. The scene is inspiring, and I get so excited by the wonder of it that I might appear to be worshipping nature or making nature an idol. However, nature in its variety of scenes and diversity of plants and animals constantly reminds me that it is God's creation. He is the One that has made it so incredibly awesome.

Nature can become an idol just like many other things. We often place our trust in the idols of this world, such as money, power, physical appearance, fame, celebrity, politics, sports, and success. We may also overemphasize family, romance, academics, leisure, food, or comfort. While these things are important, we don't want to fall into a trap of making them more important to us than God.

So, how can we tell when something is becoming an idol in our lives versus when it has its appropriate place? By making sure that our heart longs for God more than anything else. And by remembering that God is the Creator of all things. We worship Him and not the things He created.

It is crucial to pray that we don't make an idol of worldly things. We need to regularly examine our hearts. A good test is found in Matthew 6:21, "For where your treasure is, there your heart will be also." We need to pray that our "treasure" is in Jesus and not any of these other things.

Enjoy your walk in nature this week and pray that God would always be first on your mind and in your heart.

# Week 20: Coral Reefs - A Stunning Underwater Treasure of Praise

Let heaven and earth praise Him, the seas and everything that moves in them. - Psalm 69:34

"Stunning" is the word I use when I think of the underwater beauty of coral reefs. During my career as a park ranger, I travelled to Buck Island Reef National Monument, just off the coast of St. Croix Island in the U.S. Virgin Islands. It is a beautiful island with a gorgeous coral reef. The park has a snorkel trail with educational signs for the reef which identify the many different coral and tropical fish. These underwater signs provide information to snorkelers about the different types of coral and the significant plants in the reef. My job was to review the signs—someone had to do it!

My first glimpse of the reef was breathtaking. Throughout the time snorkeling, I marveled at the vibrant colors of the reef, the variety of corals, and the myriad of colorful tropical fish. I couldn't believe my eyes. What an experience! I thanked God for His great underwater creation. I couldn't help but praise Him!

This amazing underwater world makes me think of Psalm 69:34, "Let heaven and earth praise Him, the seas and everything that moves in them." The coral reef and the vibrant colors of the tropical fish in among the pure blue waters of the Caribbean Sea were so stunning, it was as though they were praising God.

Praising God communicates to God my love and appreciation of Him. I am thankful for what He has done. Singing and offering praise to God also helps shift my focus from myself to Him. Praising God helps me concentrate during my prayer time or quiet time with God by preparing my heart to hear Him more clearly. It also clears away the things that could hinder my time with Him, and helps me focus more clearly on the path ahead.

Enjoy a time in nature this week. I encourage you to start your prayer times by praising God. Sing praise to the One who created heaven and earth. This, of course, includes the stunning coral reefs!

# Week 21:   Fresh Water Springs - What's Flowing From Your Heart?

> Out of the same mouth proceed "blessing and cursing." My brethren, these things ought not to be so. Does a spring send forth fresh water and bitter from the same opening? - James 3:10-11

Many of our national parks contain hot and cold water springs as well as mineral springs. Some of these are the thermal springs of Hot Springs National Park in Arkansas, the mineral springs of Chickasaw National Recreation Area in Oklahoma, and the cold-water spring called Big Spring of Ozark National Scenic Riverways in Missouri. These springs originate from underwater sources. One park that is well known for its thermal springs is Yellowstone National Park in Wyoming. Water reaches the surface from underground in several ways, such as bubbling out as mudpots or bursting out as geysers— amazing displays of nature!

James makes reference to the untamable tongue and compares it to the waters of a spring. He states that a spring can't "send forth fresh water and bitter from the same opening." When we speak, we can't have both "blessing and cursing" coming out of our mouths. It's either one or the other. Our words, whether positive or negative, reflect what is deep down in our hearts. If selfishness, resentment, and envy are rooted deep in our hearts, they will bubble out as greed, bitterness, and jealousy. If love, joy, humility, and peace are in our hearts, they will bubble up with forgiveness, goodness, gentleness, and kindness.

We need to ask God to keep His fresh water running deep in our hearts. Then when we speak, our words will be full of grace and wisdom, not of bitterness. I frequently pray the words of the psalmist, "Let the words of my mouth and the meditation of my heart be acceptable in Your sight, O Lord, my strength and my Redeemer." (Psalm 19:14)

Enjoy your walk in nature this week. May the words of your mouth and the meditation of your heart be as a spring that sends forth refreshing water that will be a blessing to others.

# Week 22: Parks as Spiritual Sanctuaries

I will lift up my eyes to the hills—from whence comes my help? My help comes from the Lord, who made heaven and earth. - Psalm 121:1-2

The National Park Service was created by the U.S. Congress in 1916. Its mission is "to conserve the scenery and the natural and historic objects and the wildlife therein and to provide for the enjoyment of the same in such manner and by such means as will leave them unimpaired for the enjoyment of future generations." (https://www.nps.gov/grba/learn/management/organic-act-of-1916.htm) The National Park Service recognizes that its parks, in addition to being used for recreation and education, are often places for refuge and healing. People often find parks places of comfort at difficult times in their lives.

Each one of us has had periods of setbacks and disappointments in our lives. These have caused us to retreat to places to receive God's healing—emotional, physical, and spiritual. While parks are used for many activities, they can sometimes be sanctuaries for us to spend time with God.

When I visit a park, the beauty of nature reminds me that God is the Creator of all the natural features in our parks. When I find a place of solitude in nature, I "lift up my eyes to the hills" and recognize that "my help comes from the Lord, who made heaven and earth."

Take a break and escape from the hectic pace of life this week. Retreat to a place in a park and experience nature up close. This may become a spiritual sanctuary for you.

# Week 23: Rainbows - The Promise of the Holy Spirit

For the promise is to you and to your children, and to all who are afar off, as many as the Lord our God will call. - Acts 2:39

After late afternoon or early evening storms, I have seen some awesome rainbows. As a ranger, I saw rainbows over the Appalachian Mountains in Virginia, the Badlands in South Dakota, and the Grand Canyon in Arizona. Rainbows are even remarkable when arching over the skyscrapers in our urban areas or over wide expanses of the rural Midwest.

One of the most memorable rainbows I have experienced was on a family vacation to Myrtle Beach, South Carolina. After a huge rainstorm passed through, there was an incredible full-arching rainbow stretching from the beach many miles out to the ocean. Wherever you are, when rainbows appear, they are an incredible display of nature.

Rainbows also remind us of a promise from God. Genesis 9 speaks of Noah's Ark and the days of the Great Flood. After the flood had receded, and Noah stepped out of the Ark onto dry ground, God gave him a reassuring promise. Never again would the earth be destroyed by a flood. His visible sign was a rainbow—a continual reminder that God keeps His promises.

Another promise is a most precious gift from God: the Holy Spirit. Jesus stated In Luke 24:49, "Behold, I send the Promise of My Father upon you, but tarry in the city of Jerusalem, until you are endued with power from on high." So the early believers gathered in Jerusalem and received the Holy Spirit which had been promised. In Acts 2:39, Peter said of the Holy Spirit: "For the promise is to you and to your children, and to all who are afar off, as many as the Lord our God will call."

Enjoy time in nature this week. If it rains, look for a rainbow and remember God's promise of the Holy Spirit.

# Week 24: The Opossum - Finding Value

> My brothers, show no partiality as you hold the faith in our Lord Jesus Christ, the Lord of glory. - James 2:1 (ESV)

The North American opossum is a strange-looking gray marsupial seen in woods, farms, grasslands, and even suburban backyards. Most of the time, these solitary, nocturnal mammals get a bum rap. They are not seen as welcome guests. True, they are not the most attractive mammal in the world, but they are valuable to us. They can eat 5,000 ticks per season, and cockroaches, mice, and rats as well. Since they are immune to most snake venom, opossums will munch on a snake when the opportunity presents itself. Thank you very much, opossums!

Opossums remind me that in God's eyes everyone has value. Unfortunately in this world, physical appearance is highly valued. Status, bank accounts, titles, and popularity are also praised by the world. Those without these trappings can be marginalized and made to feel unworthy. We often place a lot of emphasis on status, but thankfully God doesn't!

As believers we are not to show favoritism which can lead others to feeling undervalued. No one should be made to feel unwanted or inferior to others. Everyone has value to Jesus, and they should have value to us. Even though Hollywood personalities, sports heroes, and politicians are held in high honor by many, no one needs to be a "celebrity" to be part of God's Kingdom. As Christians, we are to recognize how much God loves each person. His grace towards us is not based on our physical appearance, bank account, status, performance, or popularity. It is based on His love for us and what He did for us.

Therefore, when we are tempted to think of one person having more value than another, or even when we feel undervalued ourselves, we can think again about the undervalued opossum. We can appreciate each other based on how God values and loves each of us. "Beloved, let us love one another, for love is of God; and everyone who loves is born of God and knows God." (I John 4:7)

Enjoy a walk in nature this week. If you see an opossum, be reminded of its value and think of others that you may have undervalued. Your walk may have to be later on in the evening to see one of these nocturnal creatures, and even then they are often hard to find.

# Week 25: Joy in Nature - Waiting on the Lord

For the joy of the Lord is your strength. - Nehemiah 8:10

There is something special about being outdoors and in nature either relaxing or participating in activities such as hiking, canoeing, biking, or cross-country skiing. The exercise invigorates, and the sunshine energizes. The tranquil scenes are peaceful. We are truly able to enjoy God's creation.

Nature is also a place to pray and sense the presence of God. I am reminded of God each time I consider His creation. I gaze in wonder and give thanks for all He has made. The memories in my scrapbooks, photo albums, and digital storage of family trips and park visits as a ranger bring me back to those moments of joy. I am captivated by many scenes in nature. Here are just a few that bring me joy:

- the loftiness of the Great Smoky Mountains;
- the stately saguaro cactus of the Sonoran Desert;
- the quiet movement of ducks and geese on a Midwest pond;
- the colorful wildflowers of the tallgrass prairie; and
- the rugged rocks of the coast of Maine.

As with our time in nature, our spiritual time with God can be healing and give us renewed strength. I draw on Scriptures that speak of joy, especially during hard times. I see His beauty in the joy of worshipping and praising God. I pray that my joy in the Lord helps others see the beauty of God.

During your walk in nature this week rejoice in God's natural wonders and find that the joy of the Lord is your strength.

# Week 26:  The Tart Taste of Rhubarb - Practicing Self-Control

> For the grace of God has appeared that offers salvation to all people. It teaches us to say "No" to ungodliness and worldly passions, and to live self-controlled, upright and godly lives in this present age. - Titus 2:11-12 (NIV)

On the farm in Iowa, we had an abundance of rhubarb. When my mom asked me to go fetch a bundle of it, that meant one thing—she was going to make rhubarb pie!

Living in a farming community, everyone pretty much had the same routine. Six days a week, we got up at sunrise, tended to the cows and chickens, and worked in the fields and garden. On Sunday morning, everyone went to church, and then families gathered together for lunch and fresh homemade pies. One of those pies usually was a rhubarb pie. To this day, my sister Janelle makes rhubarb pie fresh from her garden.

With its strong tart taste, rhubarb may not seem to be an obvious choice as a dessert. But when you add lots of sugar, it makes a tasty pie. However, because of the large quantities of sugar, one slice is plenty—and now, as then, I need to show some self-control!

Whether it's too much sugar or the internet or video games or sports or social media or even the news, these things can consume us! Too much of anything can take our focus away from more important activities. Our focus should not be on the distraction of worldly things, but rather on building a relationship with Jesus and reaching out to others. Self-control is mentioned in Galatians 5:22-23: "But the fruit of the Spirit is love, joy, peace, long-suffering, kindness, goodness, faithfulness, gentleness, self-control." If we have distracting or consuming habits, we need to allow the Holy Spirit to produce the fruit of self-control in us.

Along with my cell phone, water, first aid kit, a bunch of homemade cookies, and other important provisions, I keep a Bible in my backpack. Hopefully, I spend more time with the Bible than using the cell phone or eating the cookies. I pray that I have some self-control and don't eat a whole batch at one time.

Enjoy your time in nature this week and, if you get a chance, enjoy a piece of fresh rhubarb pie. Just one piece though!

# Week 27: The Nature of Battlefields - Reconciliation and the Meaning of the Cross

And by Him to reconcile all things to Himself, by Him, whether things on earth or things in heaven, having made peace through the blood of His cross. - Colossians 1:20

While on assignment at one of our national military parks in South Carolina, Cowpens National Battlefield, a visitor approached one of the park's rangers. They had explored the battlefield grounds, but still didn't understand this American Revolutionary War site. They commented "all I see is trees and cannons." The ranger offered to take them outside and show them what he saw. He described how the two armies lined up to battle one another and the experiences of the soldiers—some afraid, some nervous, and some eager to fight. After the battle, the victorious left in victory; the defeated left in despair. The visitor nodded understanding.

The ranger had used tangible items of the battlefield, such as the trees, landscape, and artillery pieces, to paint the picture of the battle and give meaning to the intangible experiences of fear, bravery, hope, hunger, victory, and defeat.

I think about the tangible and intangible meanings of the cross. The tangibles are evident—the wooden cross, the broken body of Jesus, and His shed blood. The intangibles are reconciliation to God, the hope of salvation, and the forgiveness of sins. In the cross, I see the victory over Satan and sin, and God's never wavering love. I see the power of His blood shed for me. I also see the peace that He gave us "through the blood of His cross"—an intangible that is with me every day of my life.

As you enjoy your time in nature this week, reflect on both the tangible and intangibles aspects in nature and in your walk with Jesus.

# Week 28: Burrowing Prairie Dogs - Finding Shelter in the Most High

He who dwells under the shelter of the Most High will rest in the shadow of the Almighty. - Psalm 91:1 (NIV)

Badlands National Park in South Dakota has a variety of wildlife—the American bison, pronghorn antelope, bighorn sheep, black-footed ferrets, and prairie dogs. One morning at the park, a district ranger asked me to help inventory the bison herd. The park maintained around 500 bison and did periodic counts using a small aircraft. While flying over the park where the bison roamed, I couldn't help but notice the number of prairie dog colonies or "towns" located in the park. It was interesting to see the system of burrows they created for their homes and their protection.

The areas where prairie dogs live have many weather challenges, such as hailstorms, blizzards, floods, drought, and fires. They also have a mix of predators, including hawks, eagles, badgers, rattlesnakes, and coyotes. When an enemy is approaching, the prairie dogs produce a unique squeaky sound to alert the colony of an approaching enemy. They then scurry into the shelter of their burrows, safe from danger.

The prairie dogs' vulnerability to danger and the shelter of their burrows reminds me that God is our shelter, a refuge when we are afraid and in danger. God doesn't promise us a world free from danger, but He does gives us His help when we are in danger. "The name of the Lord is a strong tower; the righteous run to it and are safe." (Psalm 18:10) No matter what we fear or what we are facing, we can put our trust and faith in God.

When we dwell with God, we can trust that He will watch over us. When we are facing uphill battles and facing the fears of life, reading Psalm 91 is an excellent way to find the assurance of shelter during the storms of life.

Enjoy nature this week and, whether in danger or not, rest under the shelter of the Most High.

# Week 29:  A Wilted Flower - Needing Encouragement

Blessed be the God and Father of our Lord Jesus Christ, the Father of mercies and God of all comfort, who comforts us in all our tribulation, that we may be able to comfort those who are in any trouble, with the comfort with which we ourselves are comforted by God. - 2 Corinthians 1:3-4

Have you ever had a wilted plant in a flower pot or in your garden? It's an immediate reminder that the plant needs water. If we water the plant, it is remarkable how quickly it becomes upright and flourishes again. If the plant is not watered, it withers and dies.

That is true for us as well. It's amazing what a word of encouragement or a smile can do for someone. When I was a supervisor or coach and an employee or player made a mistake, I found that it was a good time to coach or instruct rather than to criticize. They already knew they had made a mistake, they didn't need to be reminded of it over and over again. What they needed was positive advice and encouragement.

Unfortunately, we are sometimes critical and unkind, rather than encouraging. At times, we become umpires or referees at heart, calling balls and strikes, and throwing penalty flags on people. Sometimes we even give critical looks or sarcastic remarks, which are quite hurtful. Instead, like water for a drooping plant, we should show others concern and encouragement—water them, not tear them down. It's amazing what a kind word or even an approving look can do. Lending a helping hand may seem such a small thing, but can make a world of difference to someone that needs a little loving attention. Lifting someone's spirits, like watering a plant, often refreshes our soul as well.

Also, at times we are like the wilted plant and are in need of encouragement from others. When we have walked through a difficult time and have known God's comfort, we are able to truly empathize with our hurting friends. We can then "comfort those who are in any trouble, with the comfort with which we ourselves are comforted by God."

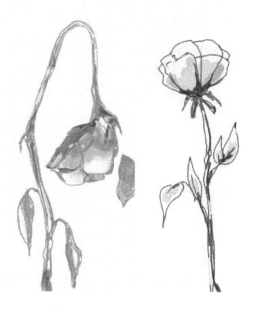

Enjoy a walk in nature this week and, if you see someone who looks a little discouraged, offer some "water" of encouragement to them.

# Week 30: Sunrise on the Seashore - His Mercies are New Every Morning

Through the Lord's mercies we are not consumed, because His compassions fail not. They are new every morning; Great is Your faithfulness. - Lamentations 3:22-23

Who of us doesn't like the seashore? I particularly like to take a brisk walk or a jog in the early morning hours along the beach at sunrise when the ocean and shore glisten with a myriad of colors. The sand under my feet may be white, golden, pink or even (in some beaches made from volcanic rock) black. The water can sparkle with colors, such as light blue-green, emerald, or deep blue. White foam can be seen on every curling wave. The sand and water seem to be painted with the many colors of the morning sky.

As the day becomes warmer, the beach is full of people soaking in the sun, reading a good book, building sand castles, playing sand volleyball, or riding bicycles. In the overnight hours, the tide comes in on the beach and goes out clearing off all evidence of the day's activities on the beach. A fresh sunrise brings a new day and a long stretch of smooth, glistening, undisturbed sand. It's like the beach is new again every morning.

Just like the beach, God's mercy, forgiveness, and grace are new every morning. I do not need to be consumed by worries and fears. God's "compassions fail not." Each day brings new hope and new opportunities to see God's grace in my life.

So remember in the early morning hours, as you start your new day, there is always a fresh "strand of smooth sand" to walk on, and a Lord whose love never fails. His mercies are indeed "new every morning."

Enjoy your walk in nature this week and, regardless if you're at the beach or not, remember that His compassions are new every morning.

# Week 31:   The Hippopotamus - Wallowing in Wetlands

A wise man fears and departs from evil, but a fool rages and is self-confident. - Proverbs 14:16

In March 2017, I had the privilege of serving on a mission team to Uganda and Rwanda. At the end of our time serving, we visited Rwanda's Akagera National Park which includes Lake Ihema, Central Africa's largest protected wetland. The landscape was stunning! We saw zebras, Cape buffalos, lions, baboons, African deer, hippopotami, and dozens of varieties of colorful birds.

Our guide at the national park was extremely knowledgable about the park ecosystem and its wildlife. He provided excellent insight on the African savannah and the wetlands of Lake Ihema. The wetlands contained a large number of hippos that swam and spent time wallowing in the mud and water to both cool off and to clean themselves. I was very impressed with their size and their movement in and around the water. The scene was amazing!

When hippos wallow, they are doing what God made them to do. However when we "wallow," we typically are choosing to stay in a place that is not God's best for us. We often justify our own "wallowing," because we have a level of comfort and familiarity with our "small" sins or self-pity or grudges. We can get caught up staying comfortable in our unwillingness to forgive, our worry, our envy, or our dislike for and disapproval of others. Things happen and people disappoint us. We form a negative opinion and sink into a "wallow" and dwell there.

The time we spend in our wallows holds us back from developing the character that God desires in us, such as forgiveness. We need to have wisdom, depart from evil, and put our confidence in Christ and not in ourselves. Sometimes that means leaving sins or thought patterns that are comfortable to us. We are called to admit our mistakes, depart from wallowing (which is sin), and, instead, move to the place God wants us to be. It's better to just leave the wallowing to the hippos!

Enjoy a time in nature this week. Escape the tendency to wallow and rather rejoice in our amazing God.

# Week 32: Preserving Greek Ruins - The Enduring History of Scripture

Heaven and earth will pass away, but My words will by no means pass away. - Matthew 24:35

One of my international assignments with the National Park Service was to travel to the seaport town of Sevastopol located on the coast of the Black Sea on the Crimean Peninsula. My job, along with two other colleagues, was to review the education operations at the well-preserved ruins of the ancient Greek port city of Chersonesos. We also offered suggestions to assist with their submission to UNESCO (United Nations Educational, Scientific and Cultural Organization) for designation as a World Heritage Area.

The 5th-century BC ruins of Chersonesos are a major tourist attraction. I was fascinated by this site that had existed during the time of the Old Testament writings, long before the birth of Christ and the missionary journeys of the Apostle Paul. It gave me a physical context for how the people in the Bible lived, worked, and played—even if what remained was only ruins.

I like thumbing through and learning about the history of each book of the Bible. I can learn about the purpose of the book, the author, the date written, to whom it was written, and the setting as well as key verses, key people, key places, and special features of the book. Reading about the history of each book gives me important background and a deeper understanding of the Bible.

I have a great appreciation for the authors inspired by God to write the books of both the Old and New Testaments. Not only that, these writings were preserved and handed down for generations until they were compiled into the Bible that we know today. I believe that the Scriptures are inspired by God.

I am thankful for those who over the centuries have kept His Word for future generations.

Enjoy your walk in nature (or at historical sites) this week. Appreciate the complete Word of God and be grateful for those inspired by God to write it and those who have preserved it for all generations.

# Week 33: Learning from Others - Listening to Jesus

My sheep hear My voice, and I know them, and they follow Me. - John 10:27

While working at an 1840s historic frontier military park in Kansas, Fort Scott National Historic Site, my supervisor asked me to give a presentation to a group of visually-impaired students ranging from 10-15 years old. As I prepared for the presentation, I laid a bison hide over a table with some historical objects next to it. Although the students couldn't see these items, they could touch them while I described them and told stories about their use.

As I talked, I noticed their concentration as they ran their fingers through the thick, soft buffalo hide. Their focus on what I said and on the bison hide was extremely keen. It seemed as though their attentiveness and insight were sharper because of their visual impairment. I closed my eyes and ran my hands through the hide as well and began to understand that sight itself could sometimes be a distraction.

A teacher once told me that when teaching about nature, she would have her students stand outside for one minute with their eyes open, but remain silent, observing all that was around them. Then she would have them close their eyes and stay silent for another minute. It was amazing how much more they observed in nature during those two minutes with their other senses.

The precious time that I had with the visually-impaired students helped me realize that because of my dependence on sight, I often experience less with my other senses. It's as if the superficial and external did not give me the full picture. John 10:27 states, "My sheep hear My voice, and I know them, and they follow Me." We are to hear the voice of our Shepherd. Yet we are often so distracted by activities, responsibilities, thoughts, and sights that we don't listen for or hear His voice. Listening is a very important aspect of both following God and understanding people. Listening well takes concentration, it can be invaluable to us in our walk with God and in communication with each other.

Take a moment to experience nature with all your senses and appreciate different aspects of God's creation this week. Also, please offer your love and support to people with disabilities.

# Week 34: Place Caution in Your Backpack - Keep Watch Over Your Heart

Be alert and of sober mind. Your enemy the devil prowls around like a roaring lion looking for someone to devour. Resist him, standing firm in the faith. - I Peter 5:8-9 (NIV)

My son and I went cross-country skiing in Grand Teton National Park in late winter. This park has magnificent views of the Teton range. Although we were enjoying our time together and the scenery, we were always mindful of our surroundings and kept alert for signs of black bears. Bear repellent and other safety devices were in our backpacks in case one did appear.

While in nature, we need to be knowledgeable about and aware of those things that can harm us. If we don't learn to recognize the "leaves of three" poison ivy, we can end up with an awful, itchy rash that can last long after a hike. We also need to be mindful of poisonous snakes that hide under rocks near a trail or coiled in a pile of wood.

As a ranger, I always told visitors that they should treat every snake as though it was poisonous and just leave it be. We also need to be aware of wild animals as we go through their habitat. Rarely do they attack people, but they can cause harm and even be deadly if they are provoked or feel that they or their family are in danger.

Just as we should watch for things in nature that could be harmful to us, we must stay alert and be aware of the devil and his devices. "A wise man fears and departs from evil." (Proverbs 14:16) In our everyday life, there are things we just need to leave alone. Satan knows our weaknesses and seeks to distract and snare us through sin that causes us and others harm. God's Word provides instructions about and insight into keeping our hearts away from these snares.

Enjoy your walk with God this week. Remain alert and watchful for dangers both physical and spiritual, and make seeking Him your priority.

# Week 35: Sea Oats and Sand Dunes - Deeply Rooted in Jesus

As you therefore have received Christ Jesus the Lord, so walk in Him, rooted and built up in Him and established in the faith, as you have been taught, abounding in it with thanksgiving. - Colossians 2:6-7

Sea oats are an interesting and beautiful part of the natural scene of the seashore. While the ocean, the beach, and the sand dunes get most of our attention, these tall, subtropical grasses provide a very important function. They catch wind-blown sand, increasing the size of and replenishing the dunes.

On the surface, the sea oats appear delicate and unable to withstand the harsh winds and hurricanes they must face. However, their roots can grow up to five feet deep, giving an unswerving foundation that provides growth to the sand dunes and stabilizes the beach.

In our Christian walk, we desire to be deeply rooted in Christ. During this devotional walk together, we have talked about many aspects of our Christian walk such as:

- worshipping God, the Creator—recognizing who He is and praising Him;
- having a grateful and thankful heart;
- spending time with Him, listening and seeking to hear His leading;
- letting Him purify our hearts;
- encouraging others in Christ; and
- prayerfully reading and thinking deeply about His Word, the Scriptures.

Becoming deeply rooted in Christ incorporates these and many other things. Just like the sea oats, we need to be rooted and grounded in our walk with God. Our lives will then be characterized by a strong and deepening relationship with Him.

Enjoy your time in nature this week deeply rooted in Jesus.

# Week 36: A Trek Up Angels Landing - Sharing Christ with Others

How beautiful upon the mountains are the feet of him who brings good news, who publishes peace, who brings good news of happiness, who publishes salvation who says to Zion, "Your God Reigns." - Isaiah 52:7

Early in my park ranger career while on an assignment at Grand Canyon National Park, I visited Zion National Park in southern Utah. In Zion, there is an interesting mountain formation high above the canyon called Angels Landing. The Angels Landing hike is a five mile round-trip trek. The last half-mile before reaching the overlook at the top is quite strenuous and very steep. Being young and adventurous (at the time), I hiked up the very narrow and incredibly steep trail to the summit. Once I got to the top, Angels Landing offered a spectacular view of the canyon and valley below. The view was absolutely breathtaking!

When something profoundly affects us, we often want to share that with others. The view from Angels Landing has been shared on innumerable social media sites because of its striking beauty and the difficulty of the trek to reach the summit. I think to myself, here I have experienced these magnificent views and this magnificent Creator. However, later when I share about my hike and the views with others, do I mention the Creator or do I just simply share about the view and leave it at that? Isaiah 52:7 speaks of the importance of communicating that our "God Reigns."

Sometimes in conversations, I find myself focusing attention on myself or on things like sports, news, politics, people, activities, accomplishments, or family. While these may have their place in our day to day conversations, how often do I share about Christ with others? I should consider it a privilege and joy to share about God and the good news of Christ's salvation.

Enjoy nature this week. Share God's amazing creation and His incredible good news with others.

# Week 37: Running a Race - Facing Adversity Head On

> Therefore we also, since we are surrounded by so great a cloud of witnesses, let us lay aside every weight, and the sin which so easily ensnares us, and let us run with endurance the race that is set before us, looking unto Jesus, the author and finisher of our faith, who for the joy that was set before Him endured the cross, despising the shame, and has sat down at the right hand of the throne of God. - Hebrews 12:1-2

I have been a distance runner for most of my life, running in races from five kilometers long to 26.2-mile marathons. I have run through parks, along rivers, around lakes, on beaches, and even up mountains (small mountains, that is). I have also run races in all kinds of weather conditions—rain, wind, snow, cold weather, overcast weather (recommended), and extreme heat (not recommended). I ran a race in a driving snowstorm in Topeka, Kansas, and when the temperature was a freezing seven degrees in La Crosse, Wisconsin. During one race in Atlanta, it rained so hard that at one point I could only see the runner directly in front of me and the two inches of water flowing over my shoes. To say the least, races like these are quite an "adventure!"

Our walk with and pursuit of God is sometimes in adverse conditions. It's difficult to run a race when we are bogged down with such weights as worry, resentment, envy, or other sins. We are hindered by their snares. Hebrews 12:1 says to "lay aside every weight, and the sin which so easily ensnares us" and "run with endurance the race that is set before us." So how do we "lay aside" or cast off the sin that entangles us? Hebrews 12:2 says that we do this "looking unto Jesus," the one who paid the price on the cross for us. Even though we have many difficulties in life, we can remember that Jesus endured so much "for the joy that was set before Him." We too can run our race by keeping our eyes fixed on what is set before us.

Enjoy your adventures in nature with Jesus this week and keep your eyes fixed on Him while you run the "race."

# Week 38: What is Going on in that Pond? - Discerning what is Beneath the Surface

Let your speech always be with grace, seasoned with salt, that you may know how you ought to answer each one. - Colossians 4:6

Although not as mesmerizing as an ocean or a lake, I find ponds compelling. I wonder what's going on below the surface of a pond. What growth, if any, is taking place in that pond? Are the plants, fish, turtles, and frogs thriving or just surviving? Is there a healthy environment in the pond or are there harmful seepages or damaging organisms? I find myself gazing at ponds not for what is happening on the surface of the pond, but for what is going on underneath.

So, what does a pond remind me of in my walk with God? When I see someone who looks downcast or worried, I wonder what is going on inside them—just like looking below the surface in a pond. What are they struggling with? What burdens are they carrying? Are they going through a medical or a financial crisis? Have they been hurt by someone?

Sometimes people who are facing challenging times may appear self-absorbed or abrupt. It may be easy for us to be dismissive or judgmental toward them. Rather than responding in kind, God calls us to speak with grace and wisdom—to "season" our speech with salt. We need to ask God to give us discernment as we seek how or when to speak, or even if to respond with words at all. Often we won't know what others are going through, however, there is One who does understand their struggles and needs. We can pray for the Holy Spirit's leading in how to offer love, support, or a prayer, and in how to point them to their source of hope—Christ Jesus.

Enjoy a walk in nature this week. As with the pond, realize that those around us may be struggling inside and need the hope that is in Jesus.

# Week 39: Check for Ticks - Keeping a Spiritual Checklist

See that no one renders evil for evil to anyone, but always pursue what is good both for yourselves and for all. - 1 Thessalonians 5:15

Nature provides lots of opportunities for sanctuary, recreation, and enjoyment. However there are harmful and unseen dangers that we need to know about. One of these is ticks. Ticks hang around in tall grass and in wooded areas, and when the opportunity presents itself, they like to hang out on us. They like to burrow part way into our skin and can cause us harm.

Just like the precautions we take for weather and wildlife as we hike in the woods, we need to take precautions for ticks. Whether it is in the woods, our time in the yard, or working in the garden, we should follow a checklist to prevent tick-borne diseases. At the beginning and end of hiking trails, parks often post warning signs like:

- Be aware that ticks can cling onto you quickly.
- Check for ticks on yourself after every time you venture into nature.
- Check your clothing, your gear, and your pets for ticks as well.
- Shower soon after being outdoors.
- Call the doctor if you get a fever or rash.

Having "checklists" in our walk with Jesus can help as well. I have a mental checklist to start out and end my day:

Morning Check:

1. Begin with a devotional reading;
2. Read and study a Scripture passage;
3. Communicate and listen to God in prayer; and
4. Place my Bible in my backpack and refer to it throughout the day.

Evening Check:

1. Did I love the Lord with all my heart today?
2. Did I show love to others today?
3. Did I thoughtfully pray and have a heart of joy today?
4. Did I follow through with my commitments?; and
5. Did I ask forgiveness of those I failed?

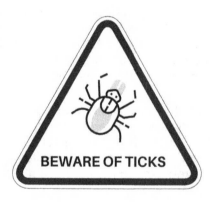

**BEWARE OF TICKS**

Enjoy your time in nature this week and always check for ticks. Keep your checklist for living in Christ handy.

# Week 40:   Autumn - God's Harvest

Then He said to His disciples, "The harvest truly
is plentiful, but the laborers are few. Therefore
pray the Lord of the harvest to send out laborers
into His harvest." - Matthew 9:37-38

Autumn is a refreshing time of year. After a long hot summer,
the weather starts getting cooler, and flocks of geese start
flying south. Who doesn't enjoy the splendor of the color in the
leaves as they start turning their brilliant reds, oranges, and
yellows? Then, after the beautiful, colorful display is almost
over and the leaves begin falling to the ground, it's time to
gather the harvest. Squirrels store acorns, farmers harvest
their crops, and we gather pumpkins and attend fall festivals.

Prior to the harvest, the ground has been prepared; the field
has been furrowed; and seeds have been planted, watered
and cared for. The Apostle Paul talks about the different
roles he and a fellow Christian named Apollos had with the
Corinthians, "I planted, Apollos watered, but God gave the
increase." (1 Corinthians 3:6)

When Jesus saw the multitudes of people (in Matthew 9),
He referred to them as a field ripe for harvest. As Christians,
we have a role in today's "harvest." As God prepares their
hearts, many people are ready to accept Jesus as their
Savior. We are to be praying and led by the Holy Spirit as we
communicate the good news of Jesus with others. We are all
called to be witnesses. Acts 1:8 says, "But you shall receive
power when the Holy Spirit has come upon you; and you shall
be witnesses to Me ... "

We can be a witness overseas or here in America—in our
cities, in our rural communities, in our offices, in our schools,

and in our neighborhoods as well as in our families. "The harvest truly is plentiful." What a joy to bring the gospel to others!

Enjoy the fall color season with a drive or hike in nature. Pray for how God wants to use you in His "harvest."

# Week 41: Kudzu - Don't Let Sin Entangle You

So I say, walk by the Spirit, and you will not gratify the desires of the flesh. - Galatians 5:16

In our national parks, one of our most important missions is to protect and care for the native species of plants, insects, and animals that make up the natural ecosystem of the park. However, there are non-native species that crop up now and then, and invade the natural ecosystem. One such invasive species is kudzu. The plant envelops trees and bushes with its vines, blocking out their access to sunlight. Controlling and destroying established kudzu plants is very difficult. It can take years of persistent work to eliminate it completely from an area. You have to constantly watch to ensure that this fast growing invasive plant doesn't return.

Kudzu reminds us of what sin does in our lives. Sin acts like a noxious weed. It wraps its ugly vines around us and blocks us from receiving the "light" of God's Word. As Christians, we need to be aware of Satan's attempts to entangle us with temptations and sins. Each of us faces temptations. We aren't being singled out. Satan even tempted Jesus, but Jesus did not sin. Temptation isn't the sin, but yielding to temptation is.

Paul tells us in 1 Corinthians 10:13, "No temptation has overtaken you except such as is common to man; but God is faithful, who will not allow you to be tempted beyond what you are able, but with the temptation will also make the way of escape, that you may be able to bear it." Satan caters to our sinful nature, tempting us where we are weakest. Therefore we need to rely on the Holy Spirit for wisdom to acknowledge our sinful desires, and then pray to chose what is right. "If we confess our sins, He is faithful and just to forgive us our sins and to cleanse us from all unrighteousness." (1 John 1:9)

Enjoy a time in nature this week and root out invasive patterns of sin. Submit to God's direction, walking by His Spirit so as not to "gratify the desires of the flesh."

# Week 42: Special Places in Nature - Meaningful Places with God

And you will seek Me and find Me, when you search for Me with all your heart. - Jeremiah 29:13

I have strong connections with places that are associated with times when God's presence was very real and personal to me. These have often been at turning points or during difficult times in my life. Some of these have have been where I sought His guidance or needed a special touch from Him. These are special places of cherished memories.

Lake Anita State Park in Iowa has been a special park to me since I was young. A view of the cove from the boat house was especially meaningful to me. I had just graduated college, unsure of my future, and I felt a special peace from God there. As a young ranger in Shenandoah National Park, Big Run Overlook became a place to offer my gratitude for God's provision for my position as a ranger. On Holmes Beach in Bradenton, Florida, I experienced God's comfort and love in a time of great personal grief. At Fire Point Overlook, a gorgeous view overlooking the Mississippi River Valley at Effigy Mounds National Monument, I heard God's calling to be a prayer warrior.

When facing decisions or needing guidance, comfort, or just a time to be alone with God, I recall these special places and moments. Sometimes I didn't recognize God's hand at the time, but later I could see that God's presence was very real. Recalling God's guidance in the past, I often hear God's wise counsel, reassurance, and direction for the present. As Psalm 77:11 says, "I will remember the works of the Lord; surely I will remember Your wonders of old."

Enjoy nature this week. Think about or find special places that have significant meaning to you and to your walk with God.

# Week 43: Lost in the Woods! - God's Help in Difficult Times

God is our refuge and strength, a very present help in trouble. - Psalm 46:1

One summer I attended a week long training course on safety at Pictured Rocks National Lakeshore. This is a beautiful shoreline along Lake Superior on the upper peninsula of Michigan. When I checked into the hotel, I inquired about hiking trails. The clerk said that there were cross-country ski trails in the woods north of the hotel that I could run on. During a lunch break I decided to go for a short jog, following the trail which was marked by painted markings on trees. As I entered the trail, the sound of jack hammers and dump trucks from a nearby construction site irritated me. I wanted a peaceful run through the woods.

At first the trees were well marked, but farther along the paint marks had worn away. Eventually I could find no more trail marks and felt like I was running in circles. I thought, "This is great, here is a park ranger attending a training course on safety, and he gets lost in the woods!" After not knowing what to do for a couple of minutes, I prayed, "Lord I need your help. Help me find my way back to the hotel." Within a couple of minutes, I heard a beeping sound not normally heard in the woods. It was a truck backing up, and I realized that it was one of the dump trucks at that construction site. I made a beeline towards the sound and got back to the hotel in time for the next lecture.

This episode reminds me that God is always with us and is "a very present help in trouble." If we seek God, He is our refuge in all situations. Psalm 32:7 states, "You are my hiding place; You shall preserve me from trouble; You shall surround me with songs of deliverance." When we are in need of God's help, we need to pray, "call a time out" for ourselves, and calm our thoughts. Then we'll be prepared to hear God's voice. God can then redirect us to the right path, even if He has to use the sound of a dump truck to help us out!

Enjoy your walk in nature this week and make Psalm 46 part of your walk.

# Week 44:  The Cleansing Action of Wetlands - The Cleansing Power of God

Therefore, having these promises, beloved, let us cleanse ourselves from all filthiness of the flesh and spirit, perfecting holiness in the fear of God. - 2 Corinthians 7:1

Wetlands are an fascinating and valuable part of our natural environment. I enjoy canoeing and birdwatching in wetland areas. Their quiet and serene beauty may not be as stunning as mountains or waterfalls, but they are vitally important.

In the amazing natural processes of God's creation, one purpose of these shallow, water-saturated areas is to cleanse the water that flows out into a larger body of water. Reeds, cattails, and waterlilies in wetland areas trap harmful contaminants before they reach the open water. Wetlands act as a filtering system to remove pollutants and sediments improving the quality of our waters. They also control erosion and provide habitat for fish and wildlife.

I will always admire a wetland not only for its cleansing action in nature, but also for its spiritual reminder of God's cleansing power in my life. Jesus' blood has the power to clean out the pollutants and sediment in my life. As I allow the Holy Spirit to work in me, I'm transformed so that a healthy stream of purity and holiness flows in me.

As the Scripture above states, "let us cleanse ourselves" from everything that contaminates "flesh and spirit." If I am entertaining negative or sinful thoughts, or considering harmful words or actions, I need to have my thoughts purified, just like the water passing through the wetlands, so that those thoughts do not cause harm to myself or others.

Enjoy the view of a wetland this week and appreciate God's cleansing action in us.

# Week 45: Wounded Trees - A Process of Healing

He heals the broken hearted, and binds up their wounds. - Psalm 147:3

Sometimes when I am hiking or jogging along a nature trail, I come across a tree that has a scar on its trunk. At some point, the tree was damaged, and, over time, it developed a scar. The scar is often on the trunk of the tree not too far from its base. As I pass by it, I notice that, in spite of the "wound," it has grown into a strong and sturdy tree.

When I observe the tree, I think of the wounds that I have received, not just the physical hurts, but also the emotional ones, often caused by someone's careless actions or hurtful statements. Even an emotional "flesh" wound can be very harmful. Scars are a natural part of the body's healing process as the body repairs the skin and other tissues. However, wounds to the "heart" often take much more time to heal. No matter what the wound, it takes time and care, and only God can truly heal it.

God's healing is a repeated theme throughout the Bible. For example, the prophet Jeremiah calls out, "Heal me, O Lord, and I will be healed; save me and I will be saved, for you are my praise." (Jeremiah 17:14) God understands our suffering and how important healing is. His comfort is often received when praying and or reading the Bible, or when talking with a trusted friend or pastor. It can also happen when spending time in nature—seeing God's handiwork can be part of God's healing work in us. Just like scarred trees, that in spite of their "wounds" grow strong and tall, so too God "heals the broken hearted, and binds up their wounds."

Enjoy your time in nature this week and notice the scars in some of the trees. May God comfort you, heal you, and make you stronger in Him.

# Week 46: The "Rush" for Gold - Our Treasure is in Gold

How much better to get wisdom than gold! And to get understanding is to be chosen than silver. - Proverbs 16:16

When I was a ranger working at Gateway Arch National Park, I enjoyed speaking to park visitors about St. Louis serving as the "Gateway to the West" and conveying the history of westward expansion in the United States. I particularly enjoyed talking about the gold rush. On January 24, 1848, when James Marshall found a pebble at Sutter's Mill near Coloma, California the rush was on. He had found gold! Many, not only from the East, but also from other parts of the world saw this as an opportunity to strike it rich!

Who wouldn't like a little gold in their financial portfolio. Money and investments have purchasing power in this world, but God has something more powerful. For Christians, it is "much better to get wisdom than gold" and to get understanding than silver. We often think that money will provide security and contentment, but this is a false placement of our trust. True "security" is found only in God.

Matthew 6:19-21 summaries this well, "Do not lay up for yourselves treasures on earth, where moth and rust destroy and where thieves break in and steal; but lay up for yourselves treasures in heaven, where neither moth nor rust destroys and where thieves do not break in and steal. For where your treasure is, there your heart will be also." While gold and silver can prove beneficial to our worldly bank account, God asks us to find our "treasure" in Him—this has a better and an eternal return.

Enjoy a walk in nature this week. Instead of "rushing" to get gold and silver, seek wisdom and understanding, and recognize that your treasure is in God.

# Week 47: A Colony of Roseate Spoonbills - A Community of Believers

So we, being many, are one body in Christ, and individually members of one another. - Romans 12:5

I enjoy watching wading birds, such as storks, herons, ibises, egrets, bitterns, and spoonbills. They usually have long legs and long necks that help them search for food in shallow waters. They often stand completely still looking for their catch and then are able to come up with lunch in a matter of seconds.

While working at Canaveral National Seashore in Florida, I was fascinated by a colony of Roseate Spoonbills, a Blue Heron, and several Snowy Egrets wading in the marshland together. The spoonbills stood out from the other wading birds because of their pink and white coloring as well as their very distinctive, spoon-shaped bills. The herons had sleek, slender bodies and gray-blue feathers. The egrets were strikingly white in the marshland.

These colonies of wading birds are a spiritual reminder that the body of Christ is a community - "We, being many, are one body in Christ." We share a bond of fellowship with other Christian believers. While we may attend different churches that have different customs or ways of worship, the body of Christ has core beliefs that include: Jesus Christ is the Son of God and is fully God, He lived a sinless life, He was crucified for our sins and rose from the dead, and we are saved by grace through faith in Him.

Being in a "community" with other Christians gives us an opportunity to worship God together and to share our hopes and challenges. As part of a community of believers, we can give and receive encouragement, agree in prayer, and be supported in our walk. "For where two or three are gathered together in My name, I am there in the midst of them." (Matthew 18:20) As a result, we develop a deep sense of belonging and a strong bond to our community—those in Christ.

Enjoy a time in nature this week and appreciate your community in Christ. I hope that someday you are able to see some colorful wading birds in a marshland.

# Week 48: Rocks of Acadia - Jesus, the Rock of our Salvation

For no other foundation can anyone lay than that which is laid, which is Jesus Christ. - 1 Corinthians 3:11

One autumn season, my family traveled to New England, visiting Rhode Island, Vermont, New Hampshire, and Maine. There were many beautiful sites, but I was especially intrigued by the rugged coastline of Maine. In Acadia National Park, we explored the rocks jutting out from the coast. They seemed to hold the often rough sea at bay. As we climbed on the rocks, I had a feeling of safety because of the firm foundation and the solidness of the rocks beneath my feet. I was reminded that Jesus is "the Rock" in our lives. "The Lord is my rock and my fortress and my deliverer; My God, my strength, in whom I will trust." (Psalm 18:2)

The Bass Harbor Head Lighthouse in Acadia National Park was built on a stone foundation in 1858 and is still in active use today. Even when steady strong winds and harsh weather hit the seacoast, the lighthouse built on the rocks stands strong.

In Luke 6:47-49, Jesus taught about those who build their house on rock and those who build their house on sand. "Whoever comes to Me, and hears My sayings and does them, I will show you whom he is like:  he is like a man building a house, who dug deep and laid the foundation on the rock. And when the flood arose, the stream beat vehemently against that house, and could not shake it, for it was founded on the rock. But he who heard and did nothing is like a man who built a house on the earth without a foundation, against which the stream beat vehemently; and immediately it fell. And the ruin of that house was great."

When we accept Jesus as our Lord and Savior and desire to live for Him, our hopes and lives are built on Him—our firm foundation. As the storms in our lives come, we have the firm foundation of Christ to hold onto.

Enjoy a walk in nature this week. Remember that our foundation in Christ is rock solid, and we can have confidence in Him.

# Week 49: Delighting in Small Wonders - Marvelous are His Works

You formed my inward parts; You covered me
in my mother's womb. I will praise You, for I am
fearfully and wonderfully made; marvelous are
Your works, and that my soul knows very well. -
Psalm 139:13-14

There are many large wonders that catch our eye as we travel
paths in nature. But I also find the small wonders in nature
fascinating. Have you ever marveled at the details of one leaf
or a tiny insect along the trail? I often stop during my hike,
fascinated by fungi, lichens, moss, or insects, and think about
their beauty and their role in nature. I examine the details of
a flower such as its petal, pistil, and stamen. These all play a
role in and are part of the life of just one flower.

At home, my wife often has her stereo microscope out on the
kitchen table, sitting down with our kids, neighbors, friends, or
any interested party, and giving insight to the incredibly minute
details of a plant or an insect. Through the study of botany
and biology, we can see even more clearly the attention God
has given to everything that He has made.

God has also given attention to every detail of how we have
been made, even before we were born. We should praise Him,
for we are "fearfully and wonderfully made." God also cares
deeply about all aspects of our lives. Luke 12:7 says, "But the
very hairs of your head are all numbered" therefore we do not
need to fear life's challenges whether large or small. When
we can grasp even a tiny bit of His care for us, we begin to
understand that we do not need to fear.

Rejoice in God this week as you enjoy the small wonders of nature and His marvelous work in you.

# Week 50:   Manatees - Developing Humility and Meekness

Do nothing out of selfish ambition or vain conceit. Rather, in humility value others above yourselves, - Philippians 2:3 (NIV)

While on ranger assignments at national seashores in the Southeast, one of the most interesting creatures I would enjoy watching was the West Indian Manatee. These peaceful creatures of the sea swim in search of plants, float to the surface when they need air, and then slowly dive back into the water below. They are very gentle mammals with no real natural predator, although humans can pose a threat when operating a motor craft too close to the manatees.

Manatees remind me of the word "humility." Humility is a godly character that I desire to have. People who are humble are gentle and are careful not to judge. They don't boast about themselves or their accomplishments. In fact, they think more of others than they do themselves.

"Meek" people are so sensitive to the Lord's leading that they quickly listen to and follow His guidance. Moses, a leader in the Old Testament, listened to God and led an entire nation out of slavery. He followed God's guidance even when it did not make sense to him and in the face of overwhelming challenges. Would you have trusted the sea to part? Yet, he was described as "very meek, above all the men which were upon the face of the earth." (Numbers 12:3 KJV)

I would like my Christian walk to be characterized by these qualities of humility and meekness. I want to be as gentle as the manatees appear and as bold in trusting God as Moses. I know that sometimes I have not shown humility and have had pride. I sometimes question the Lord's leading and have chosen to go my own way. I instead desire to walk in humility and to have a humble heart that receives and trusts God's leading.

Enjoy your walk in nature this week and walk in the strength that true humility requires.

# Week 51:  Wilderness - Set Apart

But as He who called you is holy, you also be holy in all your conduct, because it is written, "Be holy, for I am holy." - 1 Peter 1:15-16

Wilderness areas exist in many different ecosystems. They are areas that are not cultivated and not inhabited by humans. In 1964, the U.S. Congress enacted the Wilderness Act to allow for large tracts of national forests, national parks, and national wildlife refuges to be set aside as wilderness areas. These designated wilderness areas are "set apart"—natural and pristine—without any human interaction, such as roads, buildings, power lines, or landscaping.

When I think of a wilderness and its unspoiled beauty, I am reminded that I am called to keep myself as "pristine" as possible in my walk with Jesus. Holiness is a work of the Holy Spirit living in me, helping me to be set apart and to be conformed to the image of Jesus Christ. We are called to be holy in all we do.

The blood of Christ washes away our sins, but in our daily walk we frequently chose to sin. Instead, as James 4:7 states, we need to "submit to God. Resist the devil and he will flee from you." We need to resist temptation and choose obedience to God's Word.

In my life, I desire to have no tolerance for sin. I want to be free of any envy, jealousy, gluttony, lust, greed, and a whole host of other sins. Spiritually, I desire to be "set apart"—totally devoted to our Lord and Savior.

Make wilderness part of your nature experience this week and stay set apart for Christ.

# Week 52: A Place to Pray - God's Protection Over Us

So He said to them, "When you pray, say: Our Father in Heaven ..." - Luke 11:2

The main theme in this devotional book has been the value of nature in reminding us of Scriptural truths that help us overcome temptations in our lives and help us walk on God's path. As you can tell, nature is a passion for me. My relationship with Jesus is also a passion for me. So, in this last devotion, I am writing about the opportunity to reinforce our connection with God while in nature.

We connect to God through prayer. Often we go to a quiet place, and it's just us and Him for an extended time. Sometimes our prayer is a quick request in the midst of a busy day. We have this access to God because of Christ's death on the cross and His resurrection. What a privilege to go to Him in prayer!

When in nature, we may be praying to God during a sunrise over the mountains, in the afternoon desert, or at sunset on the beach. We may even be sitting on our patio deck or on our knees in own backyard. It really doesn't matter where we are, what matters most, is whose hand is over you.

There is a picture that I have treasured since childhood. It shows Jesus reaching out His hand to protect two children. When times are difficult, I have often thought of this picture, and remembered how God protects me. I also think of this picture when praying as a youth leader or for my own children. I pray for the Father to protect them and also pray the prayer Jesus gave us in Matthew 6:9-13:

Our Father in heaven, hallowed be Your name. Your kingdom come. Your will be done on earth as it is in heaven. Give us this day our daily bread. And forgive us our debts, as we forgive our debtors. And do not lead us into temptation, but deliver us from the evil one. For Yours is the kingdom and the power and the glory forever. Amen.

Enjoy your walks with Jesus this week and thank God for His protection over you.

# Conclusion

So here we are. We have come to the end of our walk. I hope that you have enjoyed our hike in nature as much as I have. I trust that you have gained some new insight into nature, and into how nature reminds us of important truths for our lives as Christians. I find God speaking to me through His creation in the everyday experiences in nature.

To conclude our walk in nature, I have just one more short story. On one of our vacations, my wife and I were walking along Holmes Beach just west of Bradenton, Florida. In the early evening, several hundred people gathered on the shore to view the sunset over the Gulf of Mexico. They watched quietly as the sun slowly set over the horizon. Amazing! God's sunsets are captivating.

I thought to myself, this scene takes place every evening not only at this beach, but on other beaches all over the world. There are also beautiful sunsets over lakes, mountains, deserts, canyons, and prairies throughout the world. It is amazing that this one aspect in nature can capture the attention of so many people. Sunsets are made available by our great and loving creator God. We are so grateful to Him for all He has made in nature.

As you continue walking in nature, stay safe on the trail and stay close to God.

# Acknowledgments

I am grateful to our Creator God who created heaven and earth, and made all things good.

Writing this devotional has been rewarding and enjoyable. However, it has also been work and would not have been possible if it wasn't for the many people who helped me all along this path.

First, I would like to thank Silvi Erwin who inspired me to write this devotional and provided the beautiful illustrations for each topic. Your enthusiasm and assistance has been greatly appreciated.

I offer a huge note of thanks to Lisa Royse and Kimberly Wollenhaupt who lent me their time, talent, and editorial skills to provide guidance, direction, book development, and edits. I could not have accomplished this without you. Also, I want to thank George Pilch who provided further advice on editing and formatting.

A devotional book needs Biblically sound spiritual advisors. My thanks go out to Bret Hicks, Marty Larsen, Andy Royse, and Butch Ruck, for their wise input.

Another "thank you" to those who provided reference photographs for the illustrations, including Sofia Wollenhaupt, Lisa Royse, Kimberly Wollenhaupt, Heather Brown, Janelle Hunsicker, and the photographers who gave public domain access to their images on nps.gov and permission-for-use from DFW Urban Wildlife.

I am grateful also for the many who have been part of shaping my life, direction, and love for God and nature. Without these, this devotional would not have been written. My mom and dad instilled in me a deep sense of love for the Lord. Ron, my twin brother, and I enjoyed the great outdoors growing up together. Although life on the farm was hard work, we still found time to have fun and enjoy nature together. Janelle, my sister, impressed me with her gardening and 4-H projects.

# Parks Referenced in the Devotions

Acadia National Park, Bar Harbor, ME (nps.gov/acad) - Week 48

Akagera National Park, Rwanda, Africa (africanparks.org) - Week 31

Badlands National Park, Interior, SD (nps.gov/badl) - Week 28

Buck Island Reef National Monument, Christiansted, St. Croix, VI (nps.gov/buis) - Week 20

Canaveral National Seashore, Titusville, FL (nps.gov/cana) - Week 47

Chickasaw National Recreation Area, Sulphur, OK (nps.gov/chic) - Week 21

Cowpens National Battlefield, Gaffney, SC (nps.gov/cowp) - Week 27

Effigy Mounds National Monument, Harpers Ferry, IA (nps.gov/efmo) - Week 2 and 42

Fort Scott National Historic Site, Fort Scott, KS (nps.gov/fosc) - Week 33

Gateway Arch National Park, St. Louis, MO (nps.gov/jeff) - Week 2 and 46

Grand Canyon Nation Park, Grand Canyon, AZ (nps.gov/grca) - Week 26

Grand Teton National Park, Moose, WY (nps.gov/grte) - Week 34

Hot Springs National Park, Hot Springs, AR (nps.gov/hosp) - Week 21

Kaieteur National Park, Guyana, South America (guyanapnc. org) - Week 1

Lake Anita State Park, Anita, IA (iowadnr.gov) - Week 42

Niagara Falls State Park, New York, USA (parks.ny.gov) - Week 1

Ozark National Scenic Riverways, Van Buren, MO (nps.gov/ onsr) - Week 21

Pictured Rocks National Lakeshore, Munising, MI (nps.gov/ piro) - Week 43

Saguaro National Park, Tucson, AZ (nps.gov/sagu) - Week 3

Shenandoah National Park, Luray, VA (nps.gov/shen) - Week 42

Tallgrass Prairie National Preserve, Strong City, KS (nps.gov/ tapr) - Week 15

Tauric Chersonesos, Sevastopol, Crimean Peninsula (whc. unesco.org) -Week 32

Victoria Falls, Zambia and Zimbabwe, Africa (victoriafalls. co.zm) - Week 1

Yellowstone National Park, Yellowstone National Park, WY (nps.gov/yell) - Week 1 and Week 21

Zion National Park, Springdale, UT (nps.gov/zion) - Week 36